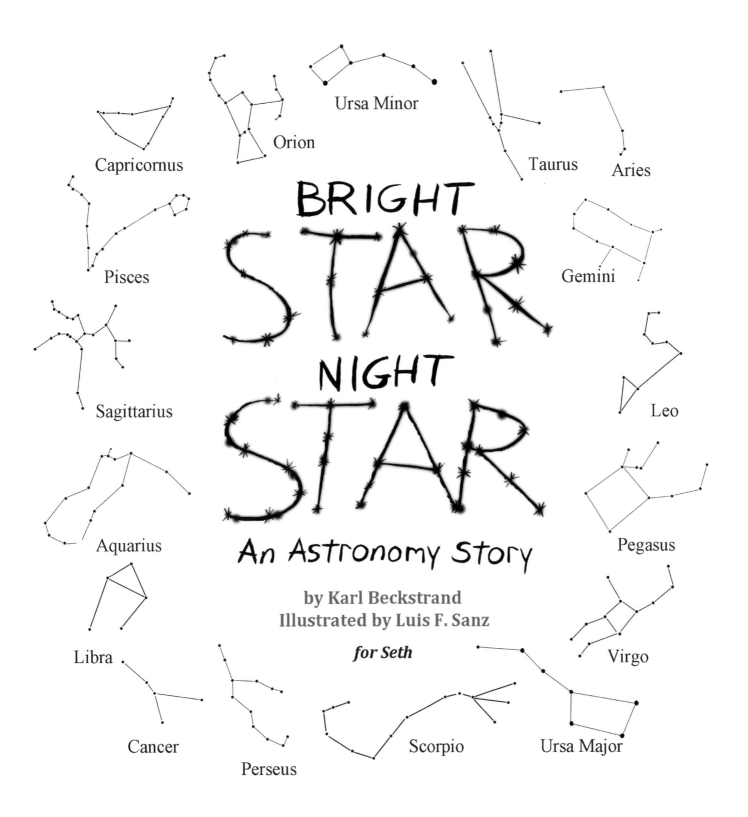

Ursa Minor

Orion

Capricornus

Taurus

Aries

Pisces

Gemini

Sagittarius

Leo

Aquarius

Pegasus

Libra

Virgo

Cancer

Perseus

Scorpio

Ursa Major

BRIGHT STAR
NIGHT STAR

An Astronomy Story

by Karl Beckstrand
Illustrated by Luis F. Sanz

for Seth

Bright Star, Night Star:
An Astronomy Story

Copyright © 2014 Karl Beckstrand and Luis F. Sanz
Premio Publishing & Gozo Books, Midvale, UT, USA
Library of Congress Catalog Number: 2013913403
ISBN: 978-0985398880, ebook ISBN: 978-1310128097

ORDER this and other adventures/ebooks via Premiobooks.com, Amazon, Baker & Taylor, Bro
EBSCO, Follett/Title Wave, Ingram, Mackin, and select ret;
Discounts available for bulk and non-profit or

Multicultural Books
by PREMIOPUBLISHING.com

FIND 17 constellations from previous page (don't forget the cover!)
Gemini, Taurus, Aries, Pisces, Perseus, Orion, Aquarius, Sagittarius, Leo,
Capricorn, Scorpio, Pegasus, Virgo, Libra, Cancer, Ursa Major (Big Dipper),
Ursa Minor (Little Dipper). Online SECRETS at PremioBooks.com

Other Premio books: *Horse & Dog Adventures in Early California; Crumbs on the
Stairs – Migas en las escaleras: A Mystery; Bad Bananas: A Story Cookbook for Kids;
Sounds in the House – Sonidos en la casa: A Mystery; Arriba Up, Abajo Down at the
Boardwalk; Anna's Prayer; She Doesn't Want the Worms! – ¡Ella no quiere los gusa-
nos! Why Juan Can't Sleep: A Mystery?* (also illustrated by Luis F. Sanz)
Libros **online books FREE**/GRATIS: **PremioBooks.com**

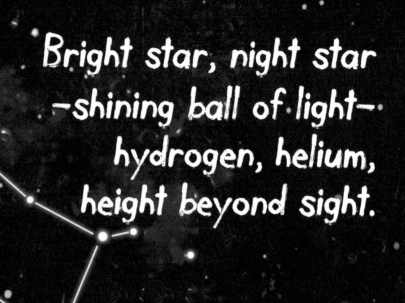

Bright star, night star
—shining ball of light—
hydrogen, helium,
height beyond sight.

Winking stars, blinking stars—
twinkling stars too—
stars have crowns we call "coronas."
Kings have crowns, do you?

Blazar, quasar, variable stars,
red stars, white stars,
Earth, moon, Mars ...

Mercury, Neptune, Jupiter, Venus, Saturn, Pluto, Europa, Uranus.

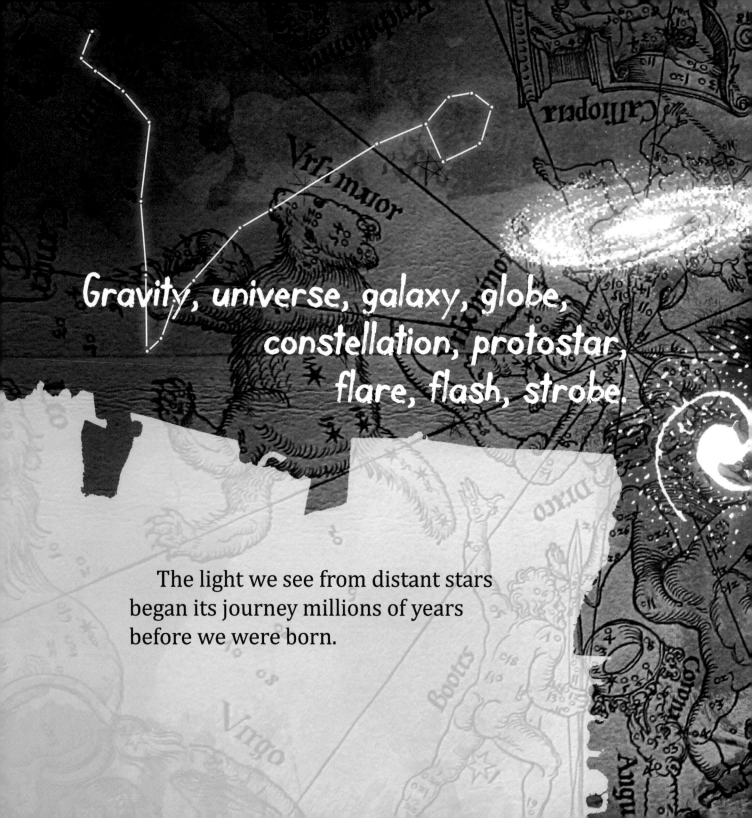

Gravity, universe, galaxy, globe, constellation, protostar, flare, flash, strobe.

The light we see from distant stars began its journey millions of years before we were born.

Our sun is a yellow star,
dark brings out its light.
Have you wished upon a star—
first one that you sight?

Star chart, star clock,
supernova, light year,
seasons, solstice, telescope, calendar.

Stars can help us find our way.
They can help us count the Mays.
Months, minutes, hours, days—
we can't make them stay.

Aurora roars, glorious—
from clouds of gas and dust—
energy, elements,
constant (we trust).

North Star, falling star,
lode star, morning star,
shell star, spinning star,
wobbly star, pulsar ...

To find the North Star, make a line between the last two stars of the Big Dipper (cup end--see cover). Follow that line up, out of the cup, to a bright star (the end of the Little Dipper handle). That star, "Polaris," shows which way is north.

Red dwarf, white dwarf,
black hole, brown dwarf,
gas giant, blue giant,
blue straggler, red giant.

Eclipse, equinox,
solar wind, and storm,
sunset, sparkling,
luminous, warm.

Glimmering, shimmering,
sunlit, soaring things—
objects on dark velvet—
fly on unseen wings.

Stars that beam, stars in stream,
seem to glow and gleam,
brilliant orbs, floating rings
in our deepest dreams.

Matter, meteor, starburst, void,
planet, comet, asteroid,
nova, nebula, neutron, night,
Milky Way, northern lights.

Fire, furnace, stars that grow—
never asking why—
cluster, luster, stars like snow,
diamonds in the sky.

(The skies are full of more stars
than you or I could count in a hun-
dred million years—dawning, dying,
and blooming anew.

Some stars live ten billion years.
But you are older than the stars.
You and I are made of stardust.
We will go on forever.)

Goodnight,

young

astronomer.

Do you think you could ever find THE END of the universe —or where it began? Is there a place in space with no stars or matter?

CPSIA information can be obtained
at www.ICGtesting.com
Printed in the USA
LVIC04n1555301114
416291LV00014B/194